Golden Lights

And Other Poems

By

Joanne P Shore

ISBN: 978-1-291-03275-8

CLASSIFICATION POETRY

Joanne P Shore

PREFACE

I was born and raised in Kidderminster, Worcestershire, England and attended Roman Catholic Schools from age 4 to16 years.

I left school to work for a short while, then I had a time of ill health after my first child and left home, to live in lodgings, I met my future husband, whose, love and kindness quite literally saved my life and my sanity, we married in 1978

I have since then had 2 more beautiful children and have also several equally beautiful grandchildren.

Back in 2001, I was diagnosed with osteo arthritis and fibromyalgia, my then, Dr told me that I had to accept it and accept the fact that I would never get any better and that I would be in wheelchair by the time I was 45, needless to say I ignored his advice and I have fought my condition every day since, I am now 53 and still not in that wheelchair.

My health issues, I also have chronic asthma, left me quite depressed and subsequent other problems caused me to go through a very difficult time.

I finally began writing my poems in approximately 2004 ,as a way to deal with my problems and to save me from having to deal with counsellors, who I found quite useless.

The poems in this book are not in chronological order or according to the time when I originally wrote them.

I hope you enjoy taking your time by reading them.

Joanne P Shore

Chapter 1

The beginning of my journey into the realms of my inner thoughts and dreams, which led to the poems that you are about to read.

Contents

1 Golden lights
2 Freedom
3 Imagine
4 Whispering breeze
5 Hidden dreams
6 The essence of love
7 Summertime
8 Welsh sunset
9 Circle of life
10 Fallen leaves, hidden tears
11 Rain
12 She
13 The willow tree
14 This rose
15 Dreams
16 Friend
17 Whispering winds
18 My friend

Golden lights

A soft glow washed over my face as I saw those golden lights
Glowing in the sky this eve as the sun was drifting
Gently down beyond the mountains way up high
For all to see that even though night has come
The sun will shine again today for me

Tomorrow, as I wake from slumber, deep
My mind will drift back to those golden dreams
Of light so soft and warm that I could feel
The love of the Almighty wrapped around
So I know that He will always be with me

Freedom

Sea breezes whisper gently, as I stand on the empty shore

My mind wanders on the past, Infinitesimal sighs, echo softly as a dove

How I long for days gone by, of happier times,

All I knew was love

All around me is silence

Soft winds blow gently across my face,

A gentle smile curves my mouth

A memory dances in my mind

Those days will come again, I'm sure

An aura of love surrounds me, so soft, secure

Shimmering round a smoky haze, shielding me from these lonely, harsher days,

So cruel, unkind, I count the days

Until love sublime, enfolds me in its gentle arms

I am free once more

Imagine

Imagine the sky wasn't blue, or the grass not green

That when we sleep at night, we did not dream our dreams

What a tragedy we'd find, in that void of our minds

If we could not remember the things that we'd felt,

People we'd loved, or taken the time

To say a kind word, to brighten a day

What would our life be if we hadn't a friend?

Who knew us so well, was always at hand

To help us along when we faltered behind

Who buoyed up our lives, when we just could not find

The way, or the light, or the wondrous joys

Those everyday pleasures that sweeten our lives

How could we survive, if we did not know love?

Of those sweetest of sounds, from the lark and the dove

Endless days; longer nights, so lonely would be

All the pleasures and sorrows, so painful today

If I did not have you to show me the way

Whispering breeze

A soft breeze sighs, through the gently swaying trees
Whispering through the canopies, of the blossom and leaves
Telling it's tales of joy, then of woe
To all who would listen, as beneath them they go
Along with their lives, whether quickly or slow

The whispering breeze echoes all of our feelings
No matter how deeply, we think they are hidden
It tells of the lovers, entwined with each other
Oblivious to all but the drum of their hearts
Beating as one that none ever can part

Who knows what it's thinking, when it sees all the lonely
The hurt, the grieving, that shed all their tears
Does it wonder what happens, to all of their fears?
Then there is laughter, so joyous, abandoned
The innocent gaiety of children at play
What more can one ask for, as dawn becomes day

Hidden dreams

In the midst of my soul a melody plays
Enhancing memories of long ago days
When all of my dreams held promise of joy
Where ever they led, my hopes sprung eternal
My aspirations, this boundless fountain of life

I meant to be great at all that I did
To bring pride, elation to all that I loved
But somewhere along the way I did falter
My mind lost its way; nothing could alter
The trembling within that caused indecision
Tearing to shreds any confidence I had

I listened with fear to the imp in my mind
When he said I was useless, I only would fail
But now I am back, with faith, with courage
To put that imp right back in it's place
To fight for those dreams buried deep in my heart
To lay the foundations for a brand new start

The essence of love

The essence of love flows within us, around us,

In the gentlest of touch, in the deepest voice

It flows through a babe in the arms of its mother,

Twines round their hearts, uplifting their souls

Echoes throughout a melodious song,

Infinite, yet fragile as a gossamer web

Swift as a bird soaring o'er the hills,

Pure as the wings of a snow white dove

Yet we still search in all the wrong places,

Wondering why it can never be found

If only we'd listen to that voice from within us,

Our hearts could find joy, our souls would know peace

Summertime

Bright rays of sun, shine down from a deep azure sky

Tracing the contours of my face, turning my skin a golden brown with its gentle heat

As I lay idly making daisy chains on the luscious deep grassy bank,

My mind's voice singing dreamily along to the melodious choir of birdsong

Filling the air with a joyous chorus, intertwining with the gently buzzing drone of bees

Drinking in the intoxicating nectar of Fairy flowers that entice ethereal butterflies to dance from petal to petal

Sleepily I dream of golden summers of yester- year as soft breezes rustle through the aged trees,

Laughing to themselves at little children playing gaily through the woods,

Their raucous chatter fighting for supremacy with the squirrels, High amid the mirriad shades of glorious green leaves

From Mother Nature's ever-changing palette of colour

Their branches heavily laden with delicious blossom bent almost ground wards

Soft as velvet dripping with delicate teardrops of the dawn dew still not quite warmed by the golden globe above

Heralding with triumphant rays, that summertime is here once more.

Welsh sunset

I set my eyes atop the towering mountain range,

Gaze with wonder, at this glorious sight above

Flaming fires, tangerine and red

Mighty dragons, as of days of yore

Frolicking amongst smoky clouds

Flames flickering, across this deep turquoise sky

Illuminating darkening shadows, of a busy town, aside the ocean down below

Candles of lamplight, float across these ever, deepening hues

Soft fluffy angels, watch over its sleepy inhabitants

Making ready for their long night's rest

Glorious dragons, paling to a soft pink glow

Golden sun slowly, lowering beyond the hills

Softening the darkness

A rosy haze shadowing the rooftops

Glistening on a gently rippling ocean below

Sinking ever deeper into the waters

Darkness overcomes, as the sun sets once more

Circle of life

In this majesty and splendour of these mountains I roam
Gazing with awe at the valleys below
Hundred foot trees, tower over this scene
Where sparkling streams, cascade down the hillsides
Bathing green fields in the waters of life
Flowing along to rivers below
That feed the seas all around this globe
Giving pleasure to all as, beside them they rest

Nestled beside them, villages and towns
Bustling with industry pleasures and pain
People within weaving webs of their lives
Filling their hearts' with joy and with woe
Circling this life 'til time immemorial
Wind roads to infinity, then back again
Praying this circle of life will not end

Fallen leaves hidden tears

I watch the leaves fall gently to the ground
Colours changed all orange and golden brown
Crackling loudly underfoot
As children gaily dance around
Making merry as they play
Their childish games all through the day

I wander back to long ago
When life for me was oh, so slow
And gentle as the fair wind blows
The weeping willow down below
That trails its branches, oh, so low

Back then I thought they didn't care
My childish dreams seemed oh so fair
That when I grew to be quite old
Like mum and dad, so I am told
My life would be so warm, not cold

I feel the tears begin to trail
Slowly as the leaves at fall
As memories gently creep within
That love was always there for me
If I had only known it then

Rain

Soft as thistledown, gently caressing velvet blossoms
Kissing deep green leaves, as it falls from downy clouds
All fluffy and white on a summers day
Rainbows arching across the sky
Casting their magnificent palette of colour
From palest yellow, to crimson bright

Sharp as a needle on a cold east wind
Biting into bright pink cheeks
Of children scurrying home from school
Chattering gaily as they run
To get inside, warm their fingers and toes
In front of a fire, so bright with flame

Lashing freely down the mountain side
Tumbling in a torrent, wild as the wind
That blows with all it's might this night
Roaring angrily in it's rage
Filling streams so high above
Their banks, until they hold no more

In all it's moods, the rain doth fall
Giving moisture to this glorious land

Of field and meadows, mountains and hills

Feeding streams and rivers below

It nourishes flowers, trees and shrubs

Enlivening all within it's wake

She

She has the sweetest soul of anyone I know

Her eyes shine out, no matter that the light

Has faded all around, where ere she goes

She makes the air around her, seem too light

As softly she does whisper sweet and low

That all she ever wants to do is paint

The clouds that form away up in the sky

Above the mountains that she roams at night

When ere all others lay their heads to sleep

She cannot understand the way she feels

Her mind can only float upon the air

That stills around her as she drifts on high

Within her dreams as quietly she prays

That once within her life she'll get to paint

The magnificence she gazed upon this day

Yet, she knows that even if she does

She can not satisfy this need within

To immortalise her feelings in this way

It doesn't matter to her that she knows

That even if she never gets to do

Another thing in life but paint this scene

Immortalise these hues of evergreen

Beneath the azure sky she looks beyond

The clouds that change their form upon the wind

That covers snowy mountain tops on high

She knows if she can do this that she'll know

The joy that fuels within her heart and soul

The willow tree

Why do you hang you're head so low

That all your pale green leaves do float

Upon the water down below

Until they feel that all they know

Just the darkness seen beneath

The waters flowing in the stream

Along the grassy banks beside

Where children play and lovers lie

Within the shade of your green leaves

So cool and dim beneath the sun

Protecting them from fiery rays

On soft and balmy summer days

Oh, gentle willow, do not weep

For all around you fondly keep

A watch for when the sun is deep

Within your branches hanging low

So soft and warm as deep within

Pale green leaves protecting them

This rose

This Rose is all that's left to remind me of you

As I sit and wonder what next to do

For all I see beyond this empty scene

In between the pictures as I lean

Towards that empty path I must take

I feel my lonely heart begin to break

Into a thousand pieces, as it shatters

I know that you will feel it does not matter

For you can only see what's in your mind

Your feelings for me now are none too kind

You said that you would not see me again

So all that I have left is just a grain

Of all the love you felt for me before

Locked deep within my soul to keep me warm

Until you let me back into your heart

Dreams

On an old wooden bridge, over a dear little stream

I stood   all alone and pondered my dream

Of what I would do, for sure it did seem

That only a while ago my mind was so clear

Of the fog that envelops it now I'm so near

To that moment I hold the one I hold dear

So close to my heart I only can fear

That   time that we lost; now you are so near

My heart races fast, I scarcely can breathe

For wonder at what I'd do if you leave

Me behind again so long I have dared

To pray you'd return, now I am so scared

That all of my dreams are clouds on the air

Friend

That sacred person you know so well

To whom, no secret you cannot tell

Who holds you up when you may fall

That makes you walk and stand so tall

Whose fire and zest brings you aglow

With light and hope when ere you go

To feel that darkness in your soul

Whose laughter shines like new spun gold

A friend who walked in parallel

With yours so that you cannot tell

Which part of you is their's as well

Whispering winds

Whispering winds, please tell me your tales

Of wondrous things, bought forth on a gale

From tropical islands to paradise land

Please tell me oh wind, of all that was planned

While blowing so gently on top of the trees

Can you tell me now, oh what did you see?

Whispering winds, did you hear the man tell

His tales of all that his Ancestors did

To make a bright life for all that he loved

Although it meant chaos, horror and flood

For though he did think that his way was first

Forgotten once more were the rules he had learned

Whispering winds, were there any bright lights

That twinkled above in the sky there at night

When all was so dark in the land here below

Could you tell me of any that still do not know?

That though they may think that the way they were taught

Was really so different than those come before

Whispering winds, do you think we might learn?

That the horrors we wrought, should never return

Can we ever find peace in this land that we love?

If only we learned from the lark and the dove

That, even so different as we all appear

Within our own hearts' we draw ever near

My friend

I feel the mist upon my mind

That steals away the thoughts I tried

To bring to life for you to know

That though you're oh so far away

You're in my thoughts all through the day

Then when the night time sinks me low

Upon my pillow this I know

That my last prayer I say each day

To keep you safe 'til I can say

My friend, you're in my heart for all of time

Chapter 2

My spiritual Journey

I have always been a person of faith, but if ever I needed it most, it was when my depression reached it's lowest ebb.

It is my belief that the following poems would not have been written if not for the guiding hand of my God

These poems are not meant to depict a particular faith or creed, but a feeling of the spirituality of all

Contents

1   Rainbows in my mind
2   Whispering breeze
3   Watch the sunrise
4   A dedication to my lord
5   Freedom from my thoughts
6   Lift me up
7   Be still and know
8   Memories
9   Flowers in the rain
10 Time
11 Spirituality
12 A smile from God
13 Blessings from God
14 I am here
15 A candle
16 Faith

Rainbows in my mind

The colours of the rainbow, though only I can see
Array themselves throughout my mind in shades of mimicry
For all the thoughts and feelings that make up this soul in me
Have blessed me with the gentle art of creativity

For when my body's wracked with pain it sends a fiery flame
Of brightest crimson through my mind and leaves a deep red blaze
That fades to orange as it cools, then palest yellow too
As my mind has told my body, pain be gone from you

When heartbreak threatens to destroy, my mind goes deepest blue
But though this colour usually is a very pretty hue
It deepens into purple shades, which, gently turn to pink
When love returns to tell me that my heart, it did not sink

Of all the colours in the rainbow of my mind it seems
The one that sets itself alone is that of coolest green
For though I often feel the sorrows of those days between
I know that I can let those sorrows ease away in dreams

Whispering leaves

The leaves whispered to me as they waved on gentle breeze

With every footstep further, you'll know that we can ease

Your way through yonder wood, up all those steps you see

Though you may think your journey is way too far to day

We know that you can do it, for we can lead the way

Just take a little step, then, take another two

For though you think you cannot, we know that you can do

This climb up through the trees where sunshine ripples through

The branches that we cling to, just as we cling to you

To help you let your courage begin to shine on through

For even though you feel it is far beyond your reach

We know that we can help you; we know that we can teach

You how to let your courage outweigh those many fears

That bound your heart so tightly, throughout those many years

So you could not let in the love to wipe those bitter tears

If only you would let us, we could give you strength

To fight the pain and sorrow that kept us at arm's length

We know that we could help you unlock that heart you keep

So tightly bound within you, buried oh so deep

For then this love we have for you will ease your soul to sleep

Watch the Sunrise

Come with me and watch the sunrise

It's rosy glow warming the earth

Radiating light from within the darkness

That enveloped the night

Let me show you how the sunlight

Brightens even the darkest shadows

Within your mind, so that all around you

Feels so bright

Even when you feel that you can't see

Hope within your heart

The sun shines through to break away that fear

And brings your soul alive

A dedication to my lord

Set my spirit free, and let it soar

Through the clear blue skies, without a cloud in sight

Show your love to me, so I can see

The radiant light within, that glows with warmth,

And fills my heart with joy

Let me know you're near to comfort me

In the dark of night, when I do pray

Guide me through the twists and turns of life

And help me see the brightness of your light

Give me faith to know that I can be

All that you expect and hope of me

Every thought and dream I have this day

I dedicate to you as I do pray

That as I sit and while away the days

That those I love are sheltered in your arms

So when united with them all again

I'll know that you'll have kept them safe from harm

Freedom from my thoughts

Find me, I am lost within my crowded thoughts

I am there, somewhere within

Search for me, I feel you can not know

How much I love you so

 Come to me, within the mirriad dreams

I dream at night for you

Tell me, what I should do, to help you find your way

Amongst the twisted web that is my mind

Help me escape this tangled web

So I can see my way

Clear a path, for me to come to you

Into the light of day

My spirit flutters madly in my mind

It wants so badly to be free

But only you can lead me through this mire

You alone can set me free

I know within my heart,

That you will answer me

My heartfelt prayer, wings its way to you

I know, deep in my soul

I will see the light of day

I feel that you will lead me to the truth

That you, are all I need to know

For peace to come to me

Lift me up

Lift me up to where my mind can see

The bigger picture that you plan for me

For just right now, I wonder where I am

In your bright land on earth, just like a lamb

I feel so lost that I may need for you

To lead me back to what I need to do

Let me know, if it is possible

For you to do so, just how far away

Are you from me, when I call on you?

To lead me through each and every day

While through a pane of glass I see the love

Of friends and family, though they cannot touch

I know that even though they love me so

Just now, they really have to show

That strength within to let me know they try

For even though within their hearts they cry

They feel the need within I have to know

They'll keep a smile upon their face right now

Help me find the courage that will be

Within me through these days that I will see

That even though they cannot be with me

In spirit I will feel their strength through Thee

When darkness overcomes my mind I'll know

That joy and light, you'll fill within my soul

Be still and know

Be still within me let me feel your grace
As in my heart I try to still this pace
For though my mind thinks it runs a race
To let you know that you are my true face

One time I wondered if you really were
Right here beside me, did you really care
If I would ever come to you untold
To rest within the arms you now unfold

I thought I was alone all of those years
When tenderness denied to me I yearned
I thought I'd done some wrong, but now I know
That all I had to do to see the glow

Of your sweet face above where no one sees
They do not know to look beyond the trees
Where darkness only broken by the stars
Hides your sweet home that lies so very far

Memories

Autumn leaves are falling softly to the ground

Children gaily playing, laughter all around

Memories flood my heart, my mind, of those childhood days

They haunt me in my lonely hours, cause the tears to flow

Those memories of wonder, childlike in its style

Of innocence so quickly lost, of gaiety of guile

Tear my very soul apart with pain for halcyon times

When all the sights, sounds and feelings I so desperately crave

Were mine to see, hear and touch to treasure to this day

Flowers in the rain

Sometimes I look at flowers in the rain

And wonder if they ever feel the pain

Of sorrows from the angels up above

Whose teardrops fall gently down with love

For all the people here on earth who try

To find a way to make the hurt go by

Without a sound uttered from their lips

When giving loved ones just a gentle kiss

They know that even if they show that pain

 That hides beneath the smile upon their face

The ones they love, simply could not try

To understand the reason why we cry

Time

If ever I had thought that life would be so short

That I would never find, the time to let you know

How much you mean to me, before it's time to go

I wonder, would I tell you that I love you so?

 Do you often wonder, what you mean to me

I know I never say the things I truly feel

Perhaps I just assume, that you can read my mind

Yet love will bind us always, until the end of time

Spirituality

What is this feeling deep inside

That even though I try to hide

My fears and sorrows, you can see

That still warm glow so bright in me?

Just like a candle flame it flares

Then bursts aflame so bright and clear

As though I know you're ever near

Me when I feel the need for thee

I often wonder how it is

That when despair enters my mind

That just a thought of you will see

A gentle calmness all entwined

For though I may not say out loud

Those thoughts enfold me in a cloud

So dense around that I may sink

Unto my mind you enter in

I feel you in those gentle times

 That, all around are wreathed in smiles

Although I may not say out loud

I know you lifted up the clouds

You bring a light into my life

And hold me gently through the night

So that I know when slumbered deep

In your strong arms my soul you'll keep

A smile from God

I smile upon you though you do not know

That I am here to tell me all your woes

To listen to you in sorrow and in joy

And help you through each and every day

You may not know that I am there with you

When pain and suffering makes you really blue

But please believe that though you cannot feel

My love for you is oh so very real

Blessings from God

When life has dealt so many blows

That you wonder where next to go

Look to your friends and you will know

The wondrous joy that still shines through

To show the light and feel the glow

Of love and friendship as you go

Throughout your daily joys and woes

Don't let your sorrows bring you down

So all you see is on the ground

Look up above to see the light

Pray to the lord with all your might

Then you will see, just as I did

That wondrous love he has to give

I am Here

When you feel yourself fall

And cannot find the strength

That you know you have

Though you may not know what length

You have to go

Before it comes to you

Though you may not think it

I will always hold you up

When you cannot see

The way through all the mist

That hides the way

From you to those who kissed

The tears away

When pain was oh so bad

You could not hear the words

I whispered to you

Even though you think

That I cannot be there

 To stop you sink

Into such deep despair

Please know I'm here

If you can let me in

To help you through

With love, we'll always win

A candle

A candle burns so brightly when all around is dark

For though we may not know it, that flames sends just a spark

Of light from high above us, where no one knows but He

Who loves us all so deeply, although we may not see

In times when we can't feel it, that love he sends back down

Can shine so bright within the flame of candles all around

To let us know that he is there, up above so high

To take the burden of our pain and set it all to flight

Faith

In my wildest imagination
I couldn't perceive
When ere I'm pain
I only would need
To turn my heart over
To you to be healed

 If only I'd known
When ere I was down
I only need turn
My mind all around
To ask you to show
The tenderest love
That you'll give to me

This love you have shown
To me o'er my life
Never did falter
Now my life is over
Despite lack of faith
You never did fail
To believe in me
Now I am come home

Chapter 3

Love

During the times of my deepest depression, the one constant in my life, was love, the love my Husband has for me and my love for him

If it wasn't for that love, particularly his love for me, I don't think I would have made it through to write this book

Contents

1   The kiss
2   Dreams
3   My love, my life
4   Eternal love
5   Love's sweet dream
6   Endless love
7   Can you tell
8   Shifting up
9   Love at first sight
10 I fell in love with a hero
11 Our love
12 My love
13 My one true love
14 Do I not love thee
15 I can feel your heartbeat
16 Love's greatest loss
17 Together again one day
18 Cast adrift

The kiss

I feel a soft warm glow within

When you press your tender lips

Even though my eyes are closed

I feel that tingle in my toes

That comes from just a single kiss

You placed on me from your sweet lips

I know that I don't often say

The things you like to hear from me

But let me tell you now my sweet

Just how your lips can burn so deep

Into my mind enthralling now

Just from that kiss upon my brow

The warmth of just that single kiss

That you have burned upon my lips

Has left me with a flame inside

That none can quench how hard they tried

For even though you left my side

The kiss remains to stem the tide

Dreams

If dreams I dreamed of you, were but mist upon the hills

That fade when summer sun turns dawn to day

If dreams were silken threads, twined through a spider's web

How long before some one would tear them down

I dream of you each night, enfolded in your arms

As if you really were right here with me

I feel your soft warm breath, drifting o'er my face

As gentle lips like velvet brush my cheek

Your voice is in my soul; I hear it as you say

How much you love me more and more each day

The longing in your mind, echoes in my heart

Wishing you could be right here with me

My dreams of you are precious, echoes from my soul

I could not bear to lose along the way

So I lock them in my heart, with a ghostly key

To cherish them until you're home again

My love, my life

I was falling

For you, though my heart never knew

How much your love would see me through

Those lonely nights

When I wondered

If my heart would stand up to all

This pain, that it would endure

For all of time

In an instant

When my life was at lowest ebb

You were there, beside me when

I felt the tears

That flowed freely

Though you knew why, you never said

Just held me close 'til they were spent

My love, my life

Eternal love

I can't tell how much I know

Of this heart of mine you stole

All those many years ago

When you told me that you loved me so

That you'd never, ever let me go

I remember oh so well

But I really cannot tell

You, how much my heart did; swell

When I heard the words you told to me

That you loved me, oh so perfectly

For I know I loved you then

More than any other one

That I'd ever love again

I could never turn to any one

Even though I spend a life alone

I'll love you, eternally

Tell you how you meant to me

All the things my heart did dream

You gave to me, unconditionally

So I'll treasure them until we meet

For our love, transcends all time

I know you'll, always be mine

In this lifetime or sometime

'Til that day, I'll always cherish thee

When our souls ascend, in perfect dreams

Love's sweet dream

Oh love's sweet dream, how I long for your sweet caress,

I crave the tenderness of your gentle kiss,

The sweetest smile, a radiant glow of a sunny morn

Oh, where is my love? enfolding me in the warmth of a love that endures

Lost in the depths of my mind

Fighting within the fluttering wings of a mirriad moths

Keeping time to the beat of my heart,

Crying out to capture the essence of your love,

An eternity of emptiness, an echoing void,

Of the loneliness that lies ahead,

Filling my heart with the cries of my soul

Endless love

Our eyes met across a crowded room
All at once, I knew you were for me
Your radiant smile set my heart aflame
With love so deep, I felt that I would drown

Your voice caressed my soul when you did speak
But words of tenderness were lost on me
I never thought you'd feel the same for me
I was so lost in endless misery

But slowly you did ease me from the brink
Of cruel despair that tore my heart in two
You showed me tender love so truly deep
Then led me as your bride along the aisle

Throughout the years you gave your love to me
I have loved you ever more each day
I couldn't wish for truer love than yours
You are my dearest love, my saving grace

Can you tell

Can you tell me how I say to you

Just how much I love you so

Can't you feel within this heart of mine

That I cannot let you go?

Can you feel the love I bear for thee

Can you feel my heart beat so?

For I love you oh so desperately

Can you not believe it's true?

I will love you 'til the end of time

I will cherish all your ways

For I cannot bear to end my life

While you can't believe my pledge

That my love for you will stand the test

Of all time this life and next

I will love you even in my death

For I know I'll see you then

When the world has come unto its end

I will see you there beyond

Then you'll know that all I said was true

I have loved you; only you

Shifting up

Shifting up, into the village, among the mountains, where I must go

For my love, is waiting yonder, where, gaily flowers, nod to and fro

Patiently, he waits to see me, as I come, slowly into his sight

With a smile, he greets me fondly, then, he hugs me, tightly

Just to show, he loves me greatly, he'll never let me go

When I was, a little younger, I used to wonder, if I would ever know

Such a love, as I have here, with my fine lover, who loves to show me so

I can feel his heart beat quickly, as he holds me, oh so tight

In his arms, I know such comfort, even in the dead of night

For I know, within his loving arms, that I can see the light

Love at first sight

You take the rose and bless it with your love

Hold my hand so gently in your own

Tell me that you'll never let me go

As you have fallen deeply for my charms

I only met you face to face this morn

Already, I can feel that I am torn

Between the heart that tells me I love you

And the head that says it can't be so

This deep devotion that I feel for you

So suddenly, I feel cannot be true

But though my head insists that this is so

I cannot bear to part myself from you

Although I know that some will call me fool

Imagining that love can come so soon

Notice, will I take of them no more

I am yours, from now for evermore

I fell in love with a hero

I was so lost when you first found me

Unable to find my way

The world around was a mystery

I didn't know the time of day

My heart was broken, torn in two

My soul a deep dark pool

I almost drowned in my despair

I sunk so low, I'm sure

Then you arrived to save the day

Lifted me up high

Above the pain and misery

Until I saw the sky

Those bright stars shining

You holding me so tight

I fell in love with a hero

 On that moonlit night

Our love

I never knew a love like yours, could come into my life

To fill my heart with joy, each time I think of you those nights

That you are far away from me, although I feel you near

For all I have to do is, see you in my mind so clear

I think of all the ways, that you have shown your love to me

In times so good and those not so, I always knew that we

Would know a love so strong and true, none ever could surpass

A love so tender, that I'd know, that it will always last

Through all the years that we have loved each other, through the tears

Joys and laughter we have known, throughout all of those years

I know that love will strengthen us, as life goes on and by

For all that we will ever have, our love will never die

Mylove

My love grows deeper with each day
That you're beside me, so I pray
That though your mind seems far away
Those memories we made, along the way
Are still within your heart and soul
That you can know, I love you so
Although you seem to wonder far
And time draws near, that we may part
I pray that you will always feel
The love we knew, throughout the years

My one true love

The gentle whisper of your tender lips
Warm breath caressing, tenderly
Strong arms surround me, in a warm embrace
My love, you fill my heart, my very soul

I long to tell you how I feel each day
When waking slowly, from a slumber deep
But you're not here my love, my light, my life
You are so very far away from me

Come home to me; enfold me in your arms
Let me beguile you with my tender charms
So when you leave me once again you take
The memory of my love to keep
You warm at night when deeply you do sleep

Do I not love thee

Do I not love thee, can you not tell,

When we speak on the phone, does my voice not swell?

When I whisper goodnight to you does it not seem

That the love I hold for you, will enter your dreams?

When you kiss me goodbye on a Monday morn

Do you not feel how my heart is torn?

For you'll be away from me all week long

Can you not hear the despair in my song?

When you come home from those days away

Do I not run to bid you good day?

With a loving smile and a hug so strong

Can you not tell I missed, you all along?

Do I not love you, surely you know

That I'd go to the ends of the earth in the snow

If you asked me, would I tell you how?

On my hands and knees, I would do it now

For my heart and soul, can no longer hold

Like a snow white rose, left out in the cold

All the love for you, though I told and told

You could not believe that I love you so

I can feel your heartbeat

I can feel your heartbeat, softly in your chest
Your strong arms hold me close, as softly your warm breath
Gently blows my hair, when you lean towards
As you drop a kiss on me, while I sleep
I can hear you whisper, to me in my dreams
That you'll always love me, even when I'm gone
You will never let, your memories of me
Fade on the horizon, when that day has come
I can feel your tender lips, soft upon my cheek
Softly they caress me, even though I sleep

Love's greatest loss

My soul torments me, as in mighty waves, crashing on the beach
Pain sears through my heart, I long to reach
Embers of a long lost love, once so filled with fire
That flamed my very being, filled me with desire

My heart still beats, as a duet, with that long lost love
Flutters gently in my breast, at the very thought
That once I loved, a love so strong
That when you went away from me,
My heart was filled with pain

The very essence of my being, cries out for your love
I long to hear your loving voice, to see your smiling face,
I long for echoes of our hearts,
To feel your warm embrace

But you are lost to me, my love, torn swiftly from my life
Now all I have are memories, of our one true love
To warm my heart, to heal my soul, to comfort me at night
Until the time when we re-unite,
In that wondrous light

Together again one day

There is a very special place in my heart, which I keep, just for you

In my soul, a light shines brightly, every single day

That I have to spend, without the love I hold so dear

A love that burns with raging fire, yet I feel the chill

Of loss so cruel, so painful, that my heart would break

But for the sure and simple faith, that sears throughout my mind

That you'll return, my love, to me, at the test of time

I long to hear those tender words of love, you used to speak

To feel the loving arms, that held me, when I did sleep

You'd whisper gently in my ear, that you'd never leave

Yet, you're gone from me, my love, I am left to plead

With all my heart, with every breath, that you'll return to me

The passion that I feel for you, will burn for ever more

Will cause the blood within my veins, to race with every thought

Of all the love that I have lost, when you were torn from me

Only your return can fill the void within my being

The empty days, lonely nights, I spend without you dear

Are just so very hard to bear, I long to hold you near

I dream of your return to me, my heart beats fast with joy

To know the strength within your arms, as you hold me tight

You tell me that you're here to stay, but then I wake to see

That all my hopes are dashed again, you are gone from me

I know that in my heart of hearts, you are gone forever

I will have to wait alone, until my life is over

When we will be united, where none can ever part

This love so deep within our souls, that's twined around our hearts.

Cast adrift

I'm cast adrift upon these lonely waves

With nought to think upon, but what has been

The mainstay of my life, until today

When all that's left are memories that play

Around my mind, while slowly I do sink

Beneath the waves of emptiness, that crush the very spirit out of me.

I long to tell you that I love you so, I crave to hear you say you love me too

My body yearns, to feel your beating heart

As crushed within your arms you'd hold me tight

You'd tell me that you'd never let me drown, beneath the weight of loneliness I feel

I'd treasure every word, that you would speak

I know if I could do it, I would keep, them locked within my heart, where they would stay

Until a time, when calmly I would let,

Them out for all to hear, how much you love me so

Chapter 4a

In honour of Service Men and Women,

past, present and future

I have always held a very deep respect for those Men and Women who serve our Country, in and out of war time.

The following few poems are written specifically to honour them

Contents

1 Always

2 When you went away

3 Angels

4 Take my hand

Always

You left your homes and families behind
To join with all the others of your kind
Who feel the need to defend people like me
Who cannot do it for ourselves you see
For though we wish we had your courage too
We don't, so you go out there for us, who
Would love to find the strength to fight along
Beside you, but you see, we're not so strong

You fight the wars that rage within this world
Sometimes you die for us, and some are hurt
But do you know how proud we are that you
Have courage and compassion so to do
So much for all of us who cannot leave
Our homes to fight beside you as you bleed
For though you may not think that we may care
May I just tell you now that we are there?

In spirit, we will fight and pray beside you
We'll ask the Lord above, so he will guide you
Back home to loved ones who are waiting there

To show you how they missed you while you were

So far away from them, oh how they worried for you

And cried for all the ones who didn't come too

For though they died in courage we shall now say

We honour you and they, for now and always

When you went away

You didn't say, when you went away

That you would not be home some day

Then all the times you wrote to me

To say that Daddy soon will be

Back here to hold me tight again

You didn't tell me what you did

When far away from me you stayed

Amongst those people who were so

Much more to you than me just now

Although you'd never tell me how

You didn't want to let me know

That fighting evil was your choice

To help the people far away

That couldn't hold the war at bay

Without you there to help today

I'm sure, if you had thought just then

That all your efforts were in vain

That you would die to help them mend

Their broken lives, they could depend

On you, to do it all again

Angels

When sorrow comes to us again and takes our breath away

Angels come to sit beside us helping us to pray

That, though this day is full of pain we know that we can say

We can make it through and live to fight another day

We may not realise that angels are beside us here

When horror all around us brings us close to fear

That maybe now is going to be the last day we will say

That we can make it through and live to fight another day

Sometimes the fighting that we do seems all too hard to bear

When all around, we see our friends in terrible despair

With bleeding wounds that some may not recover from this day

Angels spread their wings and take them home to God's sweet grace

Take my hand

Take my hand, let me lead the way

To where the Angels take your pain away

So that you'll rest in peace for many a day

Until the ones you loved can come to say

That they will join you in your time of love

Let me comfort you as I can take

You to that place so soft and full of joy

Where love belies the sadness of those days

When you were full of pain and so afraid

For all the ones you left behind today

For, though you feel so sad to leave behind

The ones you love today; let me remind

You; that they will be with you once again

When their time comes to leave this world, and then

They will be with you in your arms again

Chapter 4b

To honour those of my loved ones who have gone on to their rest

As with all of us, I have suffered the loss of a loved one on more than one occasion, the following poems are in memory of them all

Contents

1 This life
2 My love for you
3 Silence the drums
4 In dreams
5 If Heaven had a telephone

This life

This life is but a short life, yet we fail to see
How many times we miss our opportunity
To share with one another, our joys and cares until
We find that all too soon, our time is up and then
The love we tried to share is lost to us, now gone

This life is but a short life, oh, if I'd only known
That time would move so quickly, life we do not own
I would have said I love you, I would have said I cared
But now I stand alone and wonder if I dared
To ask you if you knew how much I loved you so

This life is but a short life, I never knew until
I tried to turn the clock back, so I could say to you
How much I really love you, how much you meant to me
Now you are gone forever, I am left to grieve
All that's left to say is goodbye

My love for you

My love for you I leave behind so that

You'll always have it even though we can't

Be together any more just now

But I'll be waiting 'till the time you come

To join me in this ever loving place

Where all who ever loved us give us grace

I know you'll grieve for me when I am gone

 But please remember you are not alone

My spirit stays beside you every eve

To watch and love you every hour you breathe

So that you'll know, when your time comes to join

Me, I will be right there with you again

Silence the drums

You beat your drums for us one last time yesterday

I guess you didn't realise just then, that you would play

No longer on this mortal earth; where all you loved,

Could feel the joy within you as the music fades

Although you cannot be with us no more today

For all of time, within our hearts', right there you'll stay

When sorrow threatens us, to overwhelm, we'll say

Our love for you; will never fade away

We'll wrap your memory, with twine around our hearts'

Completely with our love, so that we'll never part

With all that you have given us, while you did stay

Upon this earth although, you had to go away

Within our hearts, those drums forever beat

With love for you that time cannot defeat

No matter where, within the mists beyond

We'll find you in our thoughts forever in a song

Although for us, those drums are silent now

We know, where ever you may be, some how

You'll play once more to let us know you hear

Us, as we say our last goodbye to you right here

In dreams

Those dreams I dream of you each night

When I know I left a light

Inside my mind for you to see

That though you're just a memory

That doesn't fade, although each day

You're drifting oh so far away

I lay me down at night and say

A little prayer to wend your way

That even if I never say

How much I miss you more each day

I tell you now, how much I pray

In dreams you'll never fade away

If heaven had a telephone

Nightfall comes around so quickly, when I am alone

I wonder what you'd say right now, if only you were home

If I were just to call you, to tell you even now

To say, how much I miss you, I wish I'd told you so

How much I long to hear you voice, it seems so long ago

I wonder if I'd feel the smile, within that voice I know

If only I could hear it now, I wonder, would it show

Just once again, I'd like to say, I really love you so

Although I'm sure you always knew, I long to have a go

At telling you, if on-ly, Heaven had a telephone

Chapter 5

A little whimsicality

Although I have suffered sorrow and pain for a large amount of my life, I have also a quite whimsical nature and the following poems reflect the times of happy memories and the dreams I have for the future

Contents

1 The lark and the nightingale

2 Blue fairy

3 Spring

4 My home

5 Heralding springtime

6 I can't play the banjo

7 The legacy

8 The lake

9 Winter sunrise

10 Tranquility

11 Dawn

12 Daybreak

13 Dawn of spring

14 Gardening

The lark and the nightingale

The lark and the nightingale happened to meet

One day in the woodlands so dense and so sweet

Where the perfumes of flowers and fruits on the vines

That lark and the nightingale sang on these lines

Both songs were so silvery, delicate and clear

That all who did hear them wondered more near

To listen with joy at the tunes they carolled

In honour of all the almighty did call

Forth in this land for us all to enjoy

To treasure and care for all the long day

Blue fairy

Blue fairy whispers softly

'Please stay still while I paint thee

Such lovely fragrance will I smell

When all your petals shine brightly

For I must ply my fairy dust

To let the birds know just how much

Your bright blue colours will entice

Those bees and butterflies to light

Upon your gentle petals deep

To drink that nectar oh, so sweet'

Spring

Those dancing golden daffodils, gaze up to feel the sun

That warms the ground beneath them setting up a spark

Of tiny seeds beginning their life beneath the soil

Awakening from slumber deep when all the land was cold

They send their fragile stems above the soil to reach

The glow of sunlight brightening the aspect all around

Encouraging the buds to burst unfolding silken petals

Releasing fragrant perfume to show that spring has sprung

My home

Sleepily I gaze from my window this night
At a vision so lovely before me
The round clock face of a church steeple
Bright as the clear moonlight
Casts its dark presence over a cool night sky,
Sprinkled with a mirriad stars
Lighting up the rooftops,
Illuminating the hills

Shadows of trees pool over the cobbled streets
Empty, silent as the neighbourhood sleeps,
So peacefully
How would it be, to be un-able to see
This beauteous miracle in front of me?
I thank my Creator with all of my might
For his bountiful love that allows me this sight,
So I can sleep in God's guiding light.

Heralding springtime

Oh gentle springtime, don't you know

How much I long for you to show

That you will be along quite soon

To warm away the winter blues

Those long dark nights, incessant rain

Tapping on my window pane

Deep snow that kept me locked inside

My home for months while you did hide

I long for sunshine warm and bright

To set my heart and soul alight

I long to see those crystal colours

In raindrops left behind last night

I wish for snowdrops timidly

Peeping through the soil at me

To say that winter's on the wane

And herald springtime here again

I can't play the banjo

I can't play the banjo no matter how I try

My fingers can't pick out the notes, it really makes me cry

For I so love to hear the tunes that big old banjo sings

When others play that banjo, even in my dreams

I tried to get the music to come out how it should

But even though I made my fingers bleed, they never ever could

Get that big old banjo to sing a song for me

So I must only listen to it playing in my dreams

The legacy

Behold the mighty oak, so old, gnarled,

Yet still encompassed in the power of everlasting beauty

Translucent cobwebs, weaving their radiant silver threads amongst the boughs

Entwining through the dark, green leaves,

Sparkling in the bright sunlight

Tiny raindrops, glistening, shimmering, trembling on the brink, like tears waiting to fall

Birds nesting, singing, their voices clear as an angels' choir,

A chorus of everlasting love, echoing around

Becoming ever quieter, until just a tinkling of fairy bells

Squirrels squabbling, shattering the peace,

Stocking up the acorns for the long winter nights,

Dropping some amongst the moss below,

Leaving a forest of tiny oaks

Waiting to replace in the hush of the new dawn,

Ensuring this never ending legacy of eternal life

The lake

 Early morning sun, a golden globe amidst a clear blue sky watches over an oasis of breathless beauty

Nestled amid a mirriad hues of green

It's water smooth as glass,

Yet beneath this glossy surface

Ebbing currents cause ripples to flow

Echoing the frantic pace of paddling feet,

Belying the serenity of the graceful swans above

Whose pure white feathers cast dark shadows as they glide swiftly over the water

Oblivious to the melody of the birds singing in the trees above

Ducks squabbling over that last bit of bread that someone threw

Vying with fishermen sitting silently on the water edge, casting their lines, hoping that elusive fish will bite

Couples wander gently round, taking in the sights and sounds of this glorious morn

Reminiscing over those halcyon days of long ago

When life's pace seemed always so blissfully slow

Winter sunrise

I wander through the meadows, by the streams, o'er the hills
Wither all this beauty goes away
When autumn wind doth blow it all astray
Winter's snows lay blankets all around
Enhancing branches unadorned with leaves
Laden heavy almost to the ground

Sparkling sunshine sets it all aflame
Arising up beyond the mountain's height
Glowing brightly o'er the snowy scene
Casting light where darkness once had been
Giving warmth within my heart to see
This beauty that is all around of me

Tranquillity

Seasons come, seasons go

But none pass by, without we know

That where ere we are, our lives can show

No better sign of tranquillity

Than that of swans upon a lake,

Gliding gently over its waters

Barely rippling it's clear cold surface

Underneath this tranquil sight

None can see, with all their might

How fast doth paddle these swans' feet

To keep the serenity that we see

Who knows what thoughts are in their minds'?

When through the waters they slowly glide

If only they could tell us how

We could lead such peaceful lives

Dawn

Softly, dawn breaks on those misty hills

A cold grey blanket enveloping the air around

Covers verdant fields all shades of green

Hills and valleys below

Gently the sun comes shining through

Warm rays glowing bright

Birds send up their morning chorus

A joyful song of praise

This day so bright and clear has dawned

As night did wend its way

Daybreak

Softly lies the dawn that enters into light

When night has faded into misty air

Creates a dewy blanket, under which the flowers

And trees do wake to start another day

Brighter than the last upon this fragrant land

That we, who wander o'er it, seem to miss

When blindly we do pass upon our way

We never seem to notice, these wonders to behold

That butterflies and bees regard with joy

This beauty that surrounds us, we pass with not a blink

We take it all for granted, expect it to be there

I wonder would we miss it, if it went

Would we even notice if it was not there?

As blithely we begin another day

Dawn of spring

Still, so still lies the clear spring air

In which I sit, quietly, so serene

Not even the gentlest whisper of breeze

Tickles the slender branches of leafless trees

Standing so tall on the grassy banks

Edging a smooth, cool lake, ripple free

But for those created by great white swans

Gliding so gently under soft, milky clouds

Joyous birdsong floating way on high

In a pale blue sky, warmed by the tender spring sun

That glows so brightly over this peaceful scene

Gardening

What is this jungle I survey?

As out I look with blank dismay

At what was once a glorious scene

Of wondrous blooms and evergreen

But now I stare aghast with pain

At the devastation only rain

For months and months can obtain

I wondered how I'd ever gain

My glorious garden back again

To it's former beauty bright

Without an army and it's might

But fortunately I had help

From my beloved who did yelp

When asked to tame this wilderness

But he who always loved me best

Did comply to my request

To take the mower, strimmer too

And tame that field until anew

It once more became a lawn as new

But now it's left to me alone

To tame this wilderness I own

For though he's always my beloved

He has one fault within his head

That if a plant or tree is green

And has no bloom to be seen

Then it's a weed, it is his quest

To eradicate this pest

So to protect my precious flowers

I must toil for hours and hours

In sun and rain until again

This wild jungle has been tamed

Chapter 6

A sorrowful spirit

There are times when I look back in sorrow for all the memories I have when I wish that I could go back and change things.

However, I realise that even those times were important in that they taught me so much about myself and helped me to grow into the person I am today

Contents

1   A sorrowful spirit
2   Motherhood
3   The dream
4   Meanderings
5   Sky scape
6   Reality
7   Transcendence
8   Jealousy
9   Something
10 Missed opportunity
11 Expressions
12 Insomnia
13 Regrets
14 Long, long ago
15 Silence
16 A silent night

A sorrowful spirit

I stood so still on that moonless night

Where no one saw I looked a fright

For as my ghostly figure flowed

Surrounded by all that cloud

Where on the mountain top I weaved

A gentle pattern through the streams

Of air so high you'd only dream

That all my thoughts could let such screams

Of terror out for all to hear

Who might have listened, should they dare

Motherhood

In the very depths of my heart, hidden from the light
Is all the tortuous loneliness, the memories of your sweetness;
The childish dreams you once confessed
When you were in my arms

I loved you then with all my heart, I truly thought we'd never part
With those dark words that you relayed
You tore my soul to shreds that day
But I would never hold my heart
Away from you if you did say
That you would like to come to me
To hold me in your arms

You are my light my own sweet child
My heart's true love for you my dear
Is ever open here

The dream

I dreamed a dream last night that my past it was undone

That all I had achieved had come to naught

I dreamed I had not married, that children, I had none

My heart, it broke in pieces at the thought

That the man I love so deeply, I may have never met

The children that I bore, were now unborn

I cried such bitter tears when I thought that this was so

The anguish in my soul screamed out to mourn

I awoke from my nightmare, I realised with joy

All I thought I did not have, is truly mine

My heart's true love, I freely give, to you my dearest child

I would not change my past at any time

No matter where life takes me, or how busy I become,

You're in my thoughts today, for all of time

Meanderings

I wonder all over through valleys and dales

A picking the flowers and telling my tales

Of joy and of sorrow, of pleasure and pain

Through sunshine and moonlight, through snowfall and rain

I sit on the banks of the rivers and streams

Listening to children with their joyful dreams

Playing their games all in ones two and threes

Jumping and swimming and climbing the trees

The sigh of the rushes are soothing my mind

A drifting of blossom is gentle and kind

From birds up above comes a tuneful hello

To me as I sit on the grass down below

But all through my wonderings I couldn't relieve

My mind of the feelings you'd never believe

That all through this time I could only have one

Love of my lifetime so I must come home

Skyscape

In the chilly evening light

As I wander here this night

Gazing at the sky line up above

These wondrous hills and meadows

Lush with verdant hues

Of countless shades of green

So lush within this scene

I wonder if I ever could depart

Up above the meadows

A sky so filled with cloud

As jostling in the sky

They crowd amongst each other

So black and grey and white

Covering the light

Casting eerie shadows all around

Reality

In the misty morning light

When I've left the dark of night

Those dreams I had of you seemed, oh so real

That, even though I knew

You were not here with me

I felt your tender arms

Surround me as I sleep

And felt your soft warm breath caress my cheek

But now I am awake

I know that all my dreams

Have flown away from me

Upon the misty air and I am left

To wait alone for your return to me

Transcendence

A hush descends on me this morn

As of the day that I was born

Till silence shattered with my cries

If only I could know what lies

Ahead for me, would I know?

That is His plan for me to show

That strength of mind he gave to me

To live my life as though I see

That though my life is full of fears

Sorrow and pain, joyful tears

That come the time, I will transcend

To be with him when life must end

Jealousy

Do you believe me when I say
That you are all I ever loved
All I ever need in life
Just your happiness, I crave

Can you hear the words I say
Through the pain of jealousy
That wraps around you like a mist
Tightening ever more each day

Ghostly fingers clutching you
Around your heart, your mind, your soul
That, though I idolise you only
In your mind you're ever lonely

You I love, only you
Al I ever want to do
Is hold you in my arms and say
I adore you, I'm here to stay

Something

Something inside of me keeps dragging me back

To a place in my heart I don't want to be

I used to be free of feelings that tore

Away at my soul until they were raw

I couldn't conceive the pain that I feel

I could not believe that it was so real

Yet even though I can feel so high

With you by my side I still cannot hide

From such pain and sorrow I yearn for tomorrow

In hopes I can burrow deep within my heart

To dig out this burning and all of the yearning

That held me so strong all along

Missed opportunity

I thought I'd have another day
To say the things I want to say
But as you see it could not be
That I should say how much you mean
To me as you've been taken from
Us now before I got the chance

I didn't pick up that telephone
To call you, though I just must own
Up to the fact that I did mean
To ring you, but I let my dreams
Of other things get in the way
So I did not call you that day

I missed my opportunity
To let you know how much you mean
I really hope you can still hear
My heartfelt prayer that you are near
Enough to me that I can say
I love you rest in peace I pray

Expressions

Oh how I wish I could express, the pain that lies within my breast

That seems to tear my soul apart, with cries that pierce right through my heart

So that I wonder if I might, be able to, get through this night

Without the fear that I should see, a truly different side of me

I used to see the world so clear, and bright that it would bring a tear

To my eyes, when I would look, to see the heavens up above

I'd see the glory of the stars that twinkled all the way to Mars

And know without a doubt that He, would always be so good to me

From mortal life to rest within, the love He holds for all my kin

I hold so much within my heart, of those I loved but did depart

If only for one moment so, that I could tell them fore they go

That though I never said it then, how much I truly loved them so

Insomnia

Why is it, when all others slumber deep

My mind starts racing so I can't sleep

I think of things that I should do

But in the Morn, that sun shines through

My curtains, while my mind now thinks

Oh why must I now start to sink

Into oblivion, when all this day

I should, while sun shines, make that hay

But oh again, my heart's desire

To sleep at night when I retire

Evades me all that night, and then
Next day, I can't get up again

Regrets

If I'd known, you'd take my words to heart
I would have thought, right from the start
Just in case you're listening now
I want to tell you any how
That I did not mean, to make you go

So please come back, and let me know
That you forgive the words I said
I wish they'd stayed right in my head
I know I hurt you let me say
How sorry I am, I wish you'd stayed

I know I hurt you, yet I pray
That you'd forgive me any way
I love you now, I loved you then
I can't believe I said those things

That made you leave me all alone

Oh please, I beg you, come back home
I wish you'd heard right from the start
How much regret is in my heart
This love I have, let us please start

From the beginning, once again

Long, long ago

Long, long ago only darkness I knew

I didn't know how deep I would go

For I had lost the most precious of things

That one could lose and I didn't know

If I would ever find it again

 For I could not long endure this pain

My heart had broken, I could only feel

Emptiness now, for nothing seemed real

I wasn't sure if my life was worthwhile

For I could not even break out a smile

Then you came to me and showed me your love

I felt you closely, as soft as a dove

I have such precious love surrounding me

Showing me now, how I really feel

My life is filled now with light oh so bright

For I know now, the end of that night

That was so long, long ago now it seems

Almost as if it was in my dreams

Silence

Silence is that thunder in the brain

That resonates around and round again

Like jungle drums beating rhythmically

Telling all those thoughts of you and me

Those tales that hide behind the mask we show

To others so that they can never know

The pain and sorrows that we learn to keep

Within our hearts', we bury them so deep

Yet all the time they tremble on our lips

'Til all at once we make a little slip

Then suddenly though we may try to flee

Those secrets in our souls for all to see

And though we thought we'd hidden them so well

Our sorrows rush on forth for all to tell

That all within us really is not well

That silence clangs as loud as any bell

A silent night

Eerie stillness washes over moonlit night

Although one feels no one could come to light

The darkness that entwines you all around

Enfolding you though blanket thoughts confound

That twisted web, your mind reveals no thought

That crowds your brain to make you so distraught

To wonder whether you will ever feel

Another hand that ever felt so real

As that which touches you right now and sends

A shiver down your spine from end to end

So clammy do your own hands feel this night

You wonder what it is that gives you fright

For though the stillness of the night comes near

There really is not anything to fear

But all those thoughts within your crowded mind

Reveal the tangled web that you did bind

Of joys and sorrow, happiness and tears

From all the times within your lifetime's year

Chapter 7

The joys or otherwise of fibromyalgia

Fibromyalgia is a very difficult condition to explain to any one who has never suffered from it, even Drs have difficulty treating it, and no one seems to have any idea what causes the condition.

My own Dr once told me that there is no specific tratment for fibromyalgia and no known cure, all that She can do for me is to treat the symptoms as they occur.

The following poems I have written to try to explain what the daily life of a fibromyalgia sufferer is.

As several other conditions have symptoms that overlap those of the fibromyalgia sufferer, I feel that other people will be able to relate to these poems too

Contents

1   Release
2   If I could
3   I'm still here
4   Why?
5   Who am I
6   Fury
7   The rose
8   Please don't
9   Dance with me darling
10 Father
11 I can't hide the tears
12 Fibromyalgia blues
13 Dieting and fibromyalgia
14 There's an elephant on my legs
15 Here, beside me
16 My guardian angel
17 You won't beat me
18 Rise up Mr Phoenix
19 Storm on the horizon
20 Cleaning
21 The battle within
22 Fibro gremlin
23 Into the wilderness
24 Edge of reason
25 One flare at a time
26 Unreality

Release

Trying to conceal what you think is not real

When you know that to help you really must feel

The pain and the sorrow before you can let

It out for tomorrow you then can forget

That all of the heartache you couldn't get by

Is gone so that now you can heave, such a sigh

For only one moment, though you tried to hide

All of the little things down deep inside

That pain which you felt would not stay below

It crept through your soul so you had to show

How much you had hidden, although you did try

To keep it from slipping so you wouldn't cry

You thought that to stay strong was only the way

To help you to get by from day to day

And even when sorrow did take such a toll

That you could not see how much deep in your soul

The tendrils had tightened 'till you could not feel

How much of this heartache you tried to conceal

But now you released it so it can take flight

For ever to go out right into the night

You let all that heartache flow into the clouds

The pain and sorrow are gone from you now

So all of the love that was trying to peep

Through all of that darkness is set free to keep

If I Could

I would take the soft fresh rain to wash your tears away

And ask the summer sun to warm away your pain

I'd ask the gentle breeze to smooth your furrowed brow

And say a tender prayer, so he can show me how

My thoughts and words and deed could fill your life with ease

If it would help you know, I'd get down on my knees

To show how much I love all my friends in need

I know we live a thousand miles or so apart

But let me tell you how your words have made me start

To realise how much a friend like you can mean

Although we only see each other almost in a dream

We have to let imagination take us from this plane

So we can get to know each other, in a special way

Until the time that we can meet on that one fine day

I'm still here

You may not think I wonder

Just why I can't remember

Who you are right now

But though I don't quite know it

I really want to show that

You're a star, I know

For staying with me through this

Hard time, when I can't choose it

I still feel your love

Although I can't quite tell you

How much I still do love you

It's still real, my love

I know you wonder if I

Remember all the good times

I do too

But, though I can't recall them

Right now, I do still have them

In my heart

So, though I don't quite know you

Remember, I still love you

Love me too

Why?

Why did I think just for today?

That life would be so different than

The days before when through a haze

My mind would think that only when

A few years back I could do all

The things that I can do no more

For though my mind is still so strong

It wonders not so very long

Ago, I walked for mile on mile

I never seemed to ever tire

Although I'd lift almost all things

And even used to take a swim

But now I have to try to pace

Myself, so I won't fall on my face

My knees won't buckle under me

And oh my back, why can't I see

That, though I used to be so fit

Right now I struggle just to sit

I fight my body every day

At night, I lay me down and say

That even if I cannot do

All of those things I loved before

I will not let myself despair

For I can still climb up those stairs

Who am I?

Who am I, what am I meant to be

Is my indecision making a fool out of me

Do I not have a voice to speak out

Of all of those things that cause me to shout?

Can I not Un- twist this tongue in my head?

That wants to speak out, but feels just like lead

So it won't voice those thoughts, winding around

My mind, like a dervish spins into the ground

For though I have quite clever thoughts in my head

My voice just lets out some queer sound instead

The squeak that you hear, which makes you turn around

Could only come from me, oh, what a clown!

So, here am I caught in a spiralling whorl

Of dizzying thoughts that make my hair curl

Within my own mind, but can't seem to shout

Here I am, this is me! Oh please let me out!

Fury

What ails me that although I try
 To keep quite calm again I fly
Into a rage so high that I
Cannot control my heart and mind?

My temper I have failed to keep
Hidden in a well so deep
My fury holds me in its chains
So here I find that once again

For though inside I know that truth
How much despair I feel right now
I slowly sink into that well
That all like me can only tell

That I have hurt you, oh but my
I wish again that I could try
To keep this feeling deep inside
Although I feel I cannot hide

This pain so deep inside my mind

That tears away at all inside

To find the reason that I find

My fury won't stay down inside

The rose

Poor little rose all tattered and torn

Your soft white petals all crushed by the storm

That rages without, rain lashing down

Tearing right through the air all around

Soft velvety petals worn to the ground

Poor little rose torn by your plight

As wind blows around with all of its might

Please don't

Please don't look at me that way
I can't help if I'm in pain
So tired and low that, yet again
I had to cancel lunch today

Please don't say 'you look fine to me'
Just because you cannot see
The agony, that goes through me
Each time I hear you say

'You got your words jumbled up again'
I know, but I just can't explain
How even though I have a brain
It doesn't work out quite the same

The fog descends upon my mind
And though you think you're being kind
To me when saying exercise
I can't explain how much I tried

If only you had seen me when

I did the gardening on my bum

Because I simply couldn't stand

To dig and plant my plot of land

I'd dig out borders with a trowel

For twenty minutes, to an hour

Then oh the pain would make me howl !

And back to bed I'd have to crawl

So please remember when I say

I have a fibro flare today

That, though you cannot see my pain

It's here to bug me yet again

Dance with me darling

Dance with me darling, show me the way

Through the music let me sway

Within your arms so strong I know

That I am safe, though fast or slow

I know that I can dance with you

Your love for me will see me through

That pain I feel within my limbs

Becomes so distant as we swing

I feel your strength within my heart

As on and on we dance our part

In life's swift pageant we can move

So freely for our love does soothe

No matter that I ache each day

I feel such pain that I may cry

For when you dance with me tonight

My pain just ups and takes to flight

Through all the joys and all the pain

Through all that fog within my brain

Though sorrows fall like summer rain

My darling dance with me again

Father

Father, I know that you will always be

Beside me, when this pain takes over me

To give me strength to fight another day

So I can thank you, each night, as I pray

Father, let me tell you how I feel

Knowing you're beside me when I reel

From all that fog that takes my mind from me

And fills me with such utter misery

I know that you will help me find the courage

To dig deep into all I have in me

Within my heart and soul to tell myself

That I can make it through another day

I can't hide the tears

You follow me where I can't lead

For all who know me think they read

A smile upon my face that says

I'm fine, my life is good today

They cannot see beyond that smile

The pain that tears right though me now

That makes my body wonder if

I'll ever know a pain free day

They think if I can smile and laugh

That maybe it's not quite so bad

As I have told them many times

For all they see is that big smile

But, though I suffer pain each day

That makes me feel such misery

I try to let you off, you see

By smiling sweetly back at thee

Yet still you think you know me well

You try to say that you can tell

The truth behind that smile you see

But I can't hide the tears today

Fibromyalgia blues

My body aches, I feel so sore

My hands won't hold my cup no more

I can't remember half the things

I'm s'posed to do before the spring,

Erupts upon us with each bloom

Sparkling in the morning dew

But I will not let it beat me

This fibro blues for me you see

Must take it self away and fly

Right to the moon but I won't lie

It's going to be a battle of wits

For me to get a grip on it

Dieting and fibromyalgia

Oh pounds, why do you stick so close to me

Although I try so much to only eat

Those foods that are supposed to be so good

For this body of mine, maybe then I should

Not have to feel the pain of so much weight

Upon these poor old muscles that so ache

If only I could try some exercise

To help to make this weight of mine down size

A little dance or two maybe the key

To help me loosen up those stiffened knees

But oh so much I feel that pain once more

When I stumble up that wooden stair

A little gardening, maybe I'll try that

At least I'll get to put on my sun hat

So that the sunshine doesn't make me burn

While I try to get my frame to turn

Around so that I might Just dig that patch

Oh dear, I think I just twisted my back

They say that exercise is what we need

To help our dieting to succeed

But what they don't tell us to do is pace

So that we may manage to win this race

For once again we thing we lost that weight

But oh dear, now we have to take

A little rest in bed to help us heal

As oh how much we really hate to feel

That flame of fire that enters in our feet

To slither up our body, oh so neat

We wish we hadn't tried so hard for then

We might not have to deal with all this pain

There's an elephant on my legs

There's an elephant on my legs
And it's taken all the pain
That I really should be feeling
Pushed it to the ceiling that is my spine above

There's an elephant on my spine
And I'm sure that I'll be fine
If only it would mime
A little butterfly

There's an elephant on my legs
And I'm sure that if it knew
How much pain I'm going through
It would heave a little sigh

For though it's sitting there
Feeling oh so very sure
That it really doesn't care
If it wants to move so far

There's an elephant on my head

And it's crushing all the feeling

That, I'm sure my brain is reeling

From the pain I know I'm feeling

There's an elephant on my legs

And my spine and on my head

I am sure that if it could

Understand me; that it would

Remove itself for good

Here, beside me

Each time I feel I can no longer take
That lonesome road ahead
Whenever I think no one is there
Along this path I tread
You gently guide my faltering steps
Towards your loving arms
Showing me you'll always be
Right here within my soul

I know that you are here, beside me
With every breath I take
I feel you deep inside me
Wherever I may be
All I need to do is pray
For you will comfort me

Whenever life becomes a little hard for me
To bear the tribulation of this day, I see
All I need to do, for you to guide me through
Is lift my eyes up high, gaze beyond the sky
Knowing that, no matter what, others may say
You are there, beyond the air

To listen to my sacred prayer

For you to stay beside me, until this day is over

I know I may not feel

The answer that you give

Was that which I would really wish to hear

I hope that I am wise enough

To accept that this is so

That all that I request cannot be mine

I know that in your wisdom, you will answer me

I entrust my soul to you

I feel within my soul, whenever I need you

You're always here, beside me, as I go

Throughout my daily life, I pray I'm in your thoughts

No matter whether you are still in mine

I pray you'll walk beside me, every step I take

From now until you call me to your side

I pray you'll always love me

I feel this precious truth

Within my heart and soul when ere I pray

My guardian angel

You make me laugh, you make me cry

You make me feel that I can fly

On fragile wings I'll reach the sky

For I know if I should fall

You will be there to catch me so

That when I touch the ground again

On soft white down I'll feel no pain

You make me feel no matter when

I feel so down you'll always know

Just how to pick me up again

For even when I wonder how

To carry on you let me know

That you will always show me so

That I will feel that still warm glow

You let me know you'll always be

My special friend that I can't see

For though I know that when at night

Sometimes, I wish I could take flight

You always let me know you'll keep

A watch on me so I may sleep

You won't beat me

You give me pain so bad that I can't think

Of any means to make it go away

You make me wonder how my strength can stand

To fight against you for another day

You take my mind from me and leave a fog

That clogs my brain and turns it in a whirl

Of misty clouds resembling a log

So old and gnarled that all they do is swirl

You take my energy and make it sink

Into a mire so deep that I am stuck

Like mud so heavy that my muscles shrink

Beneath the weight and my mind runs amuck

Although I suffer all these things each day

That sometimes in my mind I like to say

Give in, accept it; let it take away

This fight in me has left me for today

But you won't win; I tell you this in truth

I'll fight today with every nail and tooth

For though, you make me suffer every day

That darn wheel chair will not be here to stay

Rise up Mr Phoenix

I do my best to try to hold you down

With pain so strong that it can make you frown

I make your limbs so heavy night and day

So you can't walk so far as yesterday

I make your brain so thick with fog so you

Can't think what it could be that you should do

But though I try to keep you down with me

Like Mr Phoenix you still rise to see

That all the things you're missing while I try

 To keep you down again can't pass you by

For longer than it takes for you to say

Rise up yon Phoenix you can fly away

Storm on the horizon

Roiling black clouds of a gathering storm move swiftly o'er the horizon

A mighty hawk with great black wings silently, hovering, Filling the air with an ominous gloom

Darkness creeps over this star less night,

No sound doth break its deathless hush

A church steeple rises above the rooftops; it's round clock face a shining beacon,

The only light in this moonless night, casting shadows with an eerie glow

A crash of thunder breaks the silence; lightning rends the sky in two

The sky opens, heaven weeps, torrents of rain lash the hillsides,

Falling on the mountain range, over the lush green fields of the valley below,

Drenching the earth, swelling streams, flooding rivers into the seas

Dawn breaks; the storm is past, peace reigns on a brand new day

Cleaning

Is it just me, oh my oh my

Can someone tell me, I wonder, why?

Just when I clean my kitchen floor

My little cats trot through the door

Or when I vacuum through the house

The front door opens and I hear a voice

Hello there mom we've come to say

Can you have the dog for us today?

I make the beds all nice and clean

Then up jumps Charlie with a grin

Makes it comfy just for him

Although I scold and scoff at him

But even as they enter in

I moan and groan it's such a pain

To have to do it all again

I think it might be me to blame

For though my home will win no show

I'll have to have another go

At cleaning house all through once more

I always let them through that door

The battle within

My world does not revolve around the whirl wind just above

Although it seems to me that it will take of all my love

For you, to keep from blowing me away within it's core

For let me tell you now, that all the days we had of yore

Will not compare to those that we will find some day again

If only I could just relieve a little of this pain

I wonder, does my body care that when it misbehaves

Your love, can give me so much strength to fight another day

For though I feel so tired when sleep eludes me yet again

One word from you, that look you give me, helps me find the way

To fight against the ravages of natures little game

To show it that with you to help, I'll fight another day

Fibro gremlin

You thought you'd take a little dig into my ribs last night

Then when I turned onto my side, to squash you, you said right

'I'll pull and twist at all her toes and let her know that she

Cannot get rid of me so easily, oh no, what can she mean!

To do with that hot water, she's filled the bath up with

Surely she can't mean to try to drown me, oh that will not do

I like to make her skin so painful that even to touch

Will make it burn with pain so very bad she will cry out

So that she cannot bear a very gentle hug from you

Who want to make her better, but you seem to only do

More harm than good, although you know you really didn't mean

To hurt her, that is all that you can do to her, it seems

I make her muscles ache so much that she can barely move

To even do a little thing like walk is hard to do

She cannot find the energy that I gleefully drained

From her, so that she cannot even help to ease the pain

To help to keep those joints and muscles supple so that she

Could exercise which, all her doctors advocate you see

I take away her memory with brain fog so that she

Cannot remember even that she meant to visit thee

Then you will get so angry with her; that fills me with glee

To see her so unhappy that she made you cross, oh mercy me!

I make her choke on silly things, like water and soft fruit

That you may take for granted, they would never worry you

So when you get so cross with her, when she is filled with pain

That even though you cannot see it, she has felt again

Those little sharp digs that I send to her to make her feel

That life is not worth living, while she feels so very ill

You may not know how much she fights to get me off her back

And out of here so that she can get her life back on track

Into the wilderness

Where did my mind go, can you see

The fog that's all around of me

That fills my brain and takes away

The simple thoughts, so I can't say

What I would like, to you today

For though I want to, they won't stay

In times not long past, I could think

Of many pleasures you and I

Have spent together night and day

When life was so much fun to play

But now, this pain has come to say

My pleasure's gone, no more today

Within this wilderness of mine

Where pain and tiredness take my time

Away from things I'd love to do

If only I could say to you

That, when this fog lifts from my brain

I'd find the words you love again

I wonder if, I am not tired

That we could rebuild all that fire

That filled our hearts' and souls' you see

For, though I am in misery

Most times, I still would like to be

That fun filled girl, I know you see

Edge of reason

Sleep eludes me yet again

My heart and soul are filled with pain

That I can never seem to gain

A grip on life that will sustain

This feeling caught inside of me

That twines around like vines have leaves

So tight that I can scarcely breathe

Oh lord when will I feel relief?

I don't recall a single thought

That I did think that you had taught

Me where to go when I was fraught

With pain and sorrow though I ought

I should have placed my trust in thee

That you were really there for me

If only I had once believed

The edge of reason be relieved

One flare at a time

Far from me now that time once spent

In youth that now I know was lent

To me so that I could have dreams

Of long ago when things just seemed

To flow beyond all thought of when

I got this thing that gives me pain

I wonder if I'd known back then

That life for me would be so changed

For though I jumped and ran with glee

Back then, my mind was oh so free

Of worries for the future now

 That took from me all of that wow

For now I cannot run and dance

My mind runs through in such a trance

This pain that sears me all aflame

Gives me such sorrow, who's to blame?

I ask myself 'most every day

My answers never ease the pain

So if I have to live this life

Where pain and muddles give me strife

For all the times I cannot think

Of what it was I had to say

Or where I put that thing today

I tell myself it's really fine

I'll take my flares one at a time

Unreality

In dreams of all I planned to do

I never thought of me and you

That we would ever fall apart

Or tear into each other's heart

I never meant to do or say

Those things that hurt the other day

Or that I ever thought of you

The way that you did say I do

I didn't think that you would see

That side of me that I can't see

The thoughts and dreams that deemed to be

A mire of unreality